A Congress WBN Publication

Produced By:

 and

DISCOVERING God TOGETHER

Discovery Workbook #7

THIS BOOK BELONGS TO:
_____

About the WE MAGNIFY YOU Discovery Workbook Series

Our families are at the core of our Kingdom Communities. The WE MAGNIFY YOU album provides us with a wonderful opportunity to develop and strengthen the expression of worship in our homes.

Each We Magnify You Discovery Workbook has been designed for parents, guardians, teachers and children to experience and explore the songs together.

Discover new sight of what it means to magnify, exalt and praise our God. Together, our families will develop a deeper and stronger understanding of who God is, releasing a whole-hearted expression of worship unto Him.

For each song on the WE MAGNIFY YOU album, we have a Workbook with the lyrics and specially created activities.

Enjoy taking time together to consider what the lyrics mean. Explore scripture verses that tell us more about each song. Engage in fun activities, including word puzzles and coloring games.

Through it all we can together gain a deeper understanding of how the words we sing reflect the lives we must live, as we align ourselves to God.

Now that is a beautiful thing!

Guidance for Parents

The WE MAGNIFY YOU worship album from Congress MusicFactory contains prayers and songs from Dr. Woodroffe and saints from Elijah Centre and Kingdom Communities across Congress WBN.

WE MAGNIFY YOU is a powerful expression of worship and praise to our Lord. Each workbook in the We Magnify You Discovery Series explores the lyrics of the songs, sharing explanations, key scriptures and fun activities.

These resources will help us to align our lives, our families and our communities to the words that we lift unto God.

GOD IS HERE (HALLELUJAH!)

LYRICS

Hallelujah! Hallelujah! Hallelujah!
The Lord our God is here!

You're here among Your people
Your glory now made known
Revealed across the nations
In majesty enthroned

Keep us pure and holy
Take us all the way
Lead us to forever
And forever we will say

Read, color and learn the verse below:

Activity Time

Hallelujah! Our Lord God is the King who rules over all. Let us be joyful and glad! Let us give Him glory!
Revelation 19:6-7

Hallelujah is a Hebrew word that means joyfully praise the Lord.

God loves it when we praise and worship Him with joyful hearts. It draws us closer to God, and Him to us.

Our worship allows God to know how we feel about Him. It also allows us to discover and know Him more.

And as we get closer to God, our joy increases and we want to honor Him even more!

Activity Time

Can you unscramble this word?

LUAHLJHLEA

_ _ _ _ _ _ _ _ _ _

Hallelujah is a really important word— it's not just praising God, but praising Him **with joy.**

Whenever we worship, let's always praise God with joy!

ANSWER: HALLELUJAH

BOOK 7: God is Here (Hallelujah)

The Lord our God is here

When we refer to God as our **Lord**, we are telling Him - and everyone else - that He is in charge of our lives.

When we declare that **our God is here,** we are acknowledging that is He is not just nearby, He is right beside us!

When our parents or teachers are right beside us, we know we have to be obedient and attentive. So, when God is beside us, we have to show, even more, how much we respect His presence, His authority and His holiness!

Activity Time

Follow the numbers and connect the dots to reveal the hidden picture. What do you see?

We lift God high, and surrender everything to Him.

BOOK 7: God is Here (Hallelujah)

You're here among Your people is the fulfilment of a promise God made a long time ago:

I will make My home with My people and live among them; I will be their God, and they shall be My people.
2 Corinthians 6:16

Your glory now made known. When God looks at His people spread across the whole earth – OBEDIENT, FAITHFUL and PURE – He sees His own character and nature reflected in them – and the world sees it too!

The reason He is with us is because we are His chosen people! We are a global company of people joyfully obeying God's commands. The Bible says this is what God always wanted!

But you are a chosen people, a royal priesthood, a holy nation, God's special possession, that you may declare the praises of Him who called you out of darkness into His wonderful light.

1 Peter 2:9

Find these words from the song hidden in the puzzle below:

☐ ENTHRONED ☐ GLORY ☐ FOREVER

☐ HERE ☐ REVEALED ☐ PEOPLE

☐ NATIONS ☐ HALLELUJAH ☐ PURE ☐ HOLY

H	E	A	L	O	T	R	R	E	U	V	O	H	L
U	E	A	E	R	R	O	L	H	R	U	T	O	H
G	E	E	N	T	H	R	O	N	E	D	P	H	L
R	E	L	A	H	E	S	S	Y	D	R	R	S	L
N	O	E	E	E	H	D	D	R	F	E	P	N	H
L	R	A	O	U	A	A	E	S	O	L	S	O	E
S	G	V	R	E	L	J	R	E	R	P	O	I	O
A	L	A	E	N	L	G	E	R	E	O	N	T	N
V	O	H	D	E	E	R	V	E	V	E	L	A	N
U	R	L	P	R	L	L	E	H	E	P	E	N	Y
E	Y	E	E	E	U	E	A	L	R	N	H	E	R
P	L	E	J	O	J	P	L	E	P	U	R	E	F
O	H	E	P	E	A	Y	E	N	E	E	R	E	E
S	L	O	E	R	H	A	D	A	Y	L	O	H	H

BOOK 7: God is Here (Hallelujah)

To **reveal** something means that it can be seen by others. God's glory is being **revealed across the nations** through us.

How do we reveal His glory?

Every time each of us—wherever we are in the world—makes the choice to:
- **LISTEN** to His Voice
- **OBEY** His Commands
- **BELIEVE** His Word
- **FOLLOW** His Ways
- **FULFILL** His Will for our lives

Psalm 96:3 Declare His glory among the nations, His marvelous deeds among all peoples.

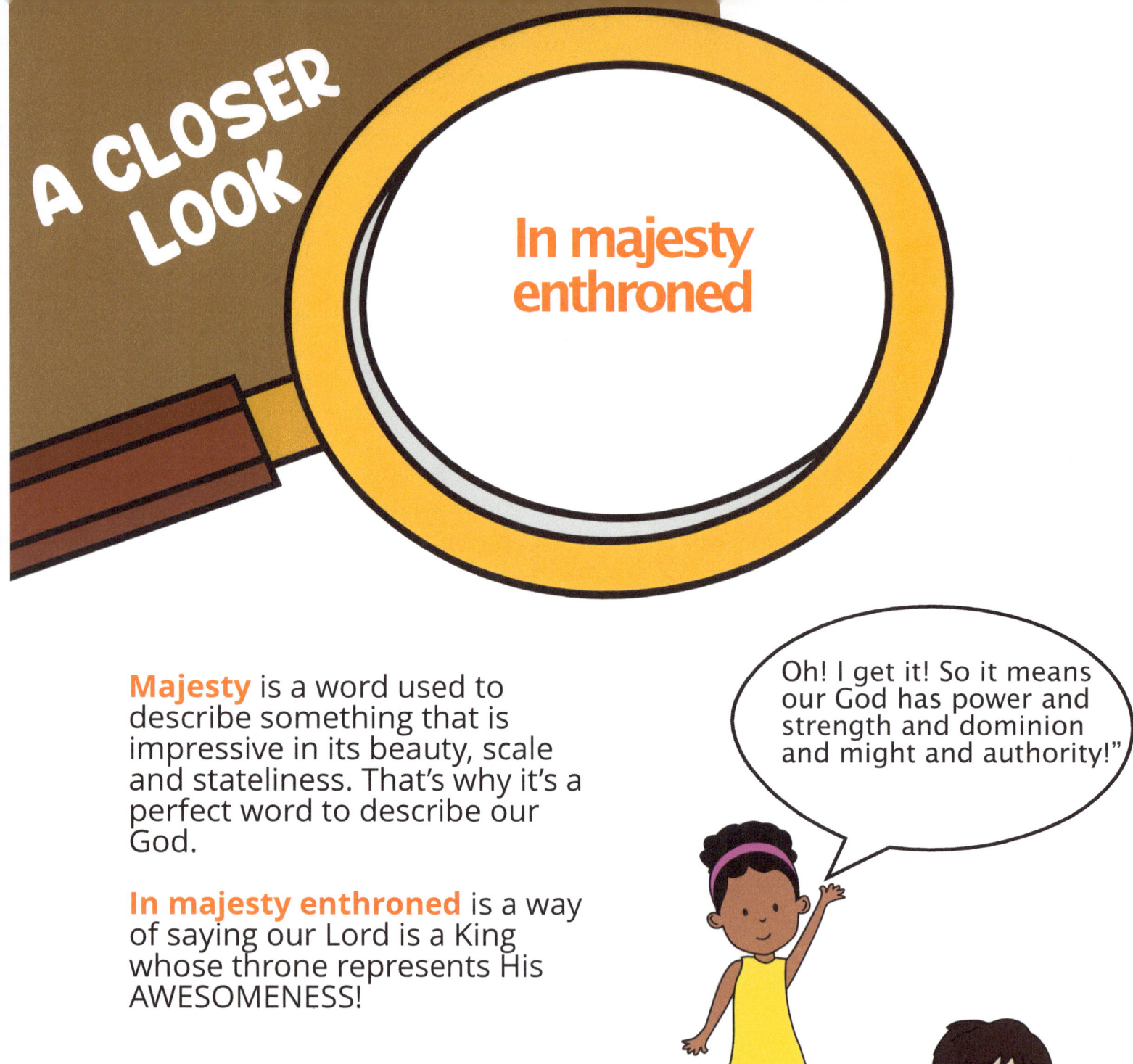

THE LORD IS MAJESTICALLY ENTHRONED!

Decorate this throne to remember God's greatness.

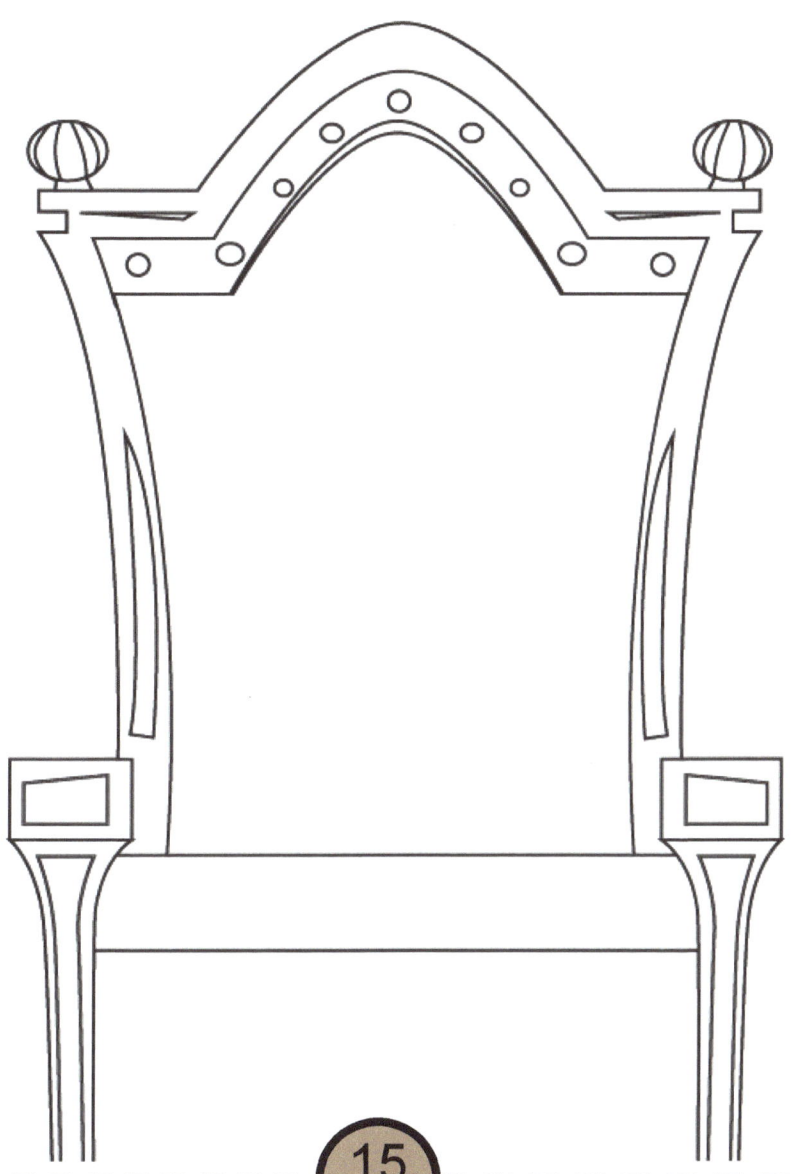

A CLOSER LOOK

Keep us pure and holy

When we say, **"Keep us pure and holy,"** we are asking the Holy Spirit to help us to give us **WISDOM** and **FAITH** and **GRACE** and **LOVE** and **STRENGTH**, so that we can stay away from what's wrong and do what is right to please the Lord.

1 Corinthians 1:30 says:

"Christ made us right with God; He made us pure and holy, and He freed us from sin."

Use the code to solve 4 hidden words and phrases that finish the statement: *"Christ has made us..."*

1. ☐☐☐☐
   11 15 12 2

2. ☐☐☐☐
   5 10 7 17

3. ☐☐☐☐☐ ☐☐☐☐
   3 12 2 2 1   3 12 10 8
   ☐☐☐
   13 6 9

4. ☐☐☐☐☐ ☐☐☐☐
   12 6 4 5 14   16 6 14 5
   ☐☐☐
   4 10 1

Secret Code

D	E	F	G	H	I	L	M	N	O	P	R	S	T	U	W	Y
1	2	3	4	5	6	7	8	9	10	11	12	13	14	15	16	17

ANSWER: PURE, HOLY, FREED FROM SIN, RIGHT WITH GOD

BOOK 7: God is Here (Hallelujah)

A CLOSER LOOK

Take us all the way
Lead us to forever
And forever we will say

Have you ever run a very long race or done something where you wondered if you could make it all the way to the end?

Well, God has a plan for His Chosen People, His Church. He has a plan for us! We want to FINISH His plan and be with Him!

So our prayer to the Lord is to **take us all the way** to completion of His plan for us and **lead us to forever,** where He is!

Forever is in eternity, meaning it has no end. I want to be with God, **FOREVER!**

WE MAGNIFY YOU Discovery Workbook Series

Draw a picture of yourself, your family and our global community all running to the finish, to forever!

Write a prayer to thank God for being with us and leading us to Forever!

BOOK 7: God is Here (Hallelujah)

MY JOURNAL

www.ingramcontent.com/pod-product-compliance
Lightning Source LLC
Chambersburg PA
CBHW041123070526
44584CB00002B/256